Charting The Path To Small Business Success

1st Edition

Jim McClaflin, EA

DesMoines-Tax.com

IMPORTANT NOTICE

iv

Contents

Chapter 1: Setting Sail On This Crazy Voyage We Call "Business"

Let's get one thing out in the open: **If you're going to start a business, you need to plan ahead.**

The main problem that new business owners have is a lack of planning and organization on their part. In addition, they too frequently try to do everything themselves, often because they think they're going to save money.

From trying to do their own bookkeeping and payroll to preparing all their own tax returns, most small business owners overestimate their own ability to stay compliant with federal, state, and local tax obligations. Many times, when they do finally come to seek help, they're two or three years down the road and they haven't done anything at all, or even worse, done it all wrong.

Unfortunately, too many new business owners stuff everything into a box and they don't remember the facts, circumstances, and situations to be able to justify potential deductions, they've lost those deductions, haven't paid their taxes for payroll, or haven't paid their personal estimated taxes.

The common element of all these situations is pretty straightforward: It's just lack of organization and lack of planning on their part.

For a typical business in this situation, getting organized should be job #1. Of course, it's better if you're organized from the get go, but even if you aren't, it's possible to recover and get back on the right track.

To start with, a business will usually need to get their books in order. A lot of times that entails pulling everything out of the boxes, the sacks, or wherever they stored things and making sense of them. Balancing their bank statements. Making sure that income is all reported, making sure their taxes are paid. Making sure that tax returns are filed. This is where it all starts.

So many times businesses get into a situation where they're payroll taxes are not being filed or their personal tax returns are not being filed. Sales tax is another issue with a lot of people, and sometimes they just don't understand how to do it. They just put it off thinking they'll go seek help "later" and "later" never comes.

Getting that bookkeeping done, getting those back tax returns taken care of and filed – these should be at the forefront of your mind if you haven't been doing this. Sometimes we have to put people on payment plans with the state or IRS to get those taxes paid. Then we must establish some sort of procedure where the books and returns are being taken care of on a regular basis.

Sometimes, small business owners are perfectly capable of doing portions of this work themselves, after a system has been set up for them. Maybe they assume the role of doing part of their own bookkeeping, such as their own invoicing, and we do the rest of it. Maybe it's a situation where we help train a spouse or part-time employee to assist in those roles, and we become their overseer for those things. Then we can pull their data in here monthly or quarterly to review it and make sure that everything is on track. Then, come tax time, we're able to get the tax return done and file timely.

The frequency at which you should work you're your professional depends on the size of your business. Some people don't have enough business for weekly or monthly service to make sense, or maybe they're seasonal and quarterly updates thus makes more sense.

For example, I have one client that's a lawn service. From April to October he's extremely busy and we have a lot of activity with his accounting and tax needs. He does his own invoicing, but my firm does the rest of his accounting. But in the winter time he really doesn't have any business, so he's planning for the next year.

He does do snow removal in the off season. Depending on the snow fall, some years it can be a lot of work, and sometimes it's almost nothing. He has a lot of time to plan for next spring and summer. For him in that off season, we're not doing a lot for him, but during his busy time we're working overtime on his behalf.

For many smaller businesses, especially home-based businesses, quarterly accounting service is more than adequate. We have clients that we perform weekly payroll for, for example. They simply drop off their receipts for expenses when they drop off hours for payroll processing, and we enter those into their bookkeeping system. Then, we schedule a quarterly review so that they know where they stand financially. At the same time, we can take care of quarterly payroll tax returns and any other personal financial and tax matters.

One of the biggest decisions that a business owner needs to make is what form of business entity to set up. We'll go into further detail on this topic in chapter two, but let's touch on it briefly here.

First off, let's clarify one thing. In the world of partnerships and LLCs, the differences can be minor, depending on where you're located. For example, here in Iowa they're one and the same, basically. Some states don't recognize an LLC so you have to know what your state recognizes. For us here in Iowa, and in most places, a LLC and partnership are one and the same. We can have single entity LLCs which are equivalent to a sole proprietor, in which they're just filing a schedule C on their personal tax return.

The advantage to having an LLC, of course, is that it

limits the liability of the owner of the company to the assets of the LLC. Somebody that would try to sue that business or that business owner can only attach the assets of the LLC -- they can't go after the assets of the owners personally.

As far as taxes go, the simplest way for a person to be in business is as a sole proprietor. Either a sole proprietor as a LLC or a sole proprietor as a non-LLC. This choice depends on what liability they have attached to their type of business.

If you have a partner, meaning you're business with somebody else, then you have to be something else. You can't be a sole proprietor. You have to be a partnership, an S corporation, or a C corporation. C corporation is the most complicated. They also pay the highest tax rates. There are cases when their taxes could be lower at lower income, and they're also the most flexible when it comes to things like fringe benefits, retirement plans, etc. I kind of discourage C corporations mostly because we don't see very many business where the C corporation would be really advantageous. If you have more than one hundred shareholders, than you have to be a C corporation.

The things that we deal with mostly are partnerships, LLCs, and S Corps. The big difference between those two entities is the S-corp requires that the officers of the company receive a W-2 at the end of the year, or other words they're on payroll. Any dollars left over at the end of the year, whether it's positive or negative dollars, pass through to the shareholders' personal tax return as either a profit or a loss that is taxed as ordinary income.

In the case of a partnership, any profits are passed through and taxed as self-employment income. Therefore, in partnership situations, you have to be on top of your personal tax planning throughout the year. These partners must make estimated tax payments periodically through the year. Of course, if the partner reports a loss, then that potentially offsets other income on the tax return or creates a net operating loss.

Partnerships can have an unlimited amount of partners, and S corporations are limited to one hundred members or shareholders. C Corporation can have unlimited shareholders.

Let's talk about established businesses that want to reduce their business taxes. If you have your books in order, proper payroll system in place, and are on top of what your taxes, there are things you can do to minimize your tax burden that are completely legal.

To start off with, depending on the type of business you operate, we'll ask a few critical questions.

What kind of equipment might they need? Have we taken advantage of the Section 179 deductions and purchased things that you need going forward? If so, let's maximize our utilization of the tax laws. For example, historically, section 179 deductions were limited to $25,000. Lately they've been at about half a million dollars, though. That's a big plus for a business owner, especially somebody who needs to purchase some major equipment. Maybe they can go ahead and make that purchase even though they may be buying it on time with a loan, but they can expense it immediately and reduce their tax liability for this year.

One simple way to reduce your tax burden is to accelerate payment of expenses into this year. If we're getting down to December and we have bills that really aren't due until January, let's get them paid in the current year so that we can deduct them in the current year. If we have the ability to delay receipt of income, perhaps by waiting to invoice customers, let's do that as well. Some businesses have the luxury of being able to do that, and some don't. They're able to tell their customers, "Don't pay me until next year." That way, we don't recognize that income in the current year.

Retirement planning for the shareholders is another big one. You see a lot of self-employed people that have zero retirement plans in place. They have not looked out towards what they're going to do however many years down the road when they're looking at retiring. They just haven't thought that far ahead. Whether it's a SEP plan, a solo 401k, or something as easy as an IRA, those are definitely good strategies to start thinking about. Even if we start out simple with them and get aggressive with them as we go, something is better than nothing.

We also like to conduct a financial analysis of what our clients are spending money on. For example, you might be spending money unnecessarily on some expenses. Maybe they're taking credit cards and they're getting charged huge fees for the privilege of accepting those credit cards. There are ways to reduce expenses, but unfortunately it's going to raise tax liability. Maybe, at the end of the year we do a bonus to the owners of the company or maybe even to key employees, to help reduce some of that income. Those are some ways to reduce your taxable income.

I would be remiss if I didn't at least briefly touch on the audit situation here in Iowa. The income tax audit is unpredictable, whether you're at the Federal or the state level. Iowa has become fairly aggressive lately about income tax audits, particularly with sole proprietors.

Sometimes, it's not very apparent why they're pulling a particular tax return and looking at it. Much of the time they are actually asking for everything. Not necessarily electronic files, but they want copies and receipts for everything that's on the return. As long as somebody has their documentation, then usually it's really easy and quick close to the audit without a lot of conversation with the auditor. We pass on the information that they're asking for (*and only what they're asking for!*), and if they feel that it's adequate they close the audit and you're done.

The biggest things that the state of Iowa is doing right now happen to be sales tax audits and trying to classify contractors as employees. These two have tripped up a lot of people lately, especially in the past year or two. Let me quick you an example.

One client that I'm working with contracts with a major nationwide company to do flooring installation. Then his company further sub-contracts to different installers. Most of these other installers are business entities on their own. They don't work exclusively for my client, they work for multiple people. In order to work for my client, they have to undergo passing a background check and other things with the major company that's hiring. When they show up on sites they're not wearing uniforms or identification that is of my client or themselves, they're wearing the identification and uniform of the nationwide company.

The state has had an extremely hard time understanding that concept. For my guy, these are truly sub-contractors. They're not employees. They don't work for him exclusively, they work for many people. They go out and find their own work, also. However, look at it from the side of the national company: Their background checks and their application process that they have to pass and go through in order to work, and it's their identification that they're using when they show up at a client site, could potentially signal that they are employees.

Many construction companies that have historically paid sub-contractors are getting challenged right now with proving that they're sub-contractors versus employees.

The other big thing is sales tax audits. If you have any kind of a business that potentially produces sales tax, there may be an inquiry. Sometimes it's easily explained away, sometimes it's not. Sometimes you find out that things aren't really what they appear to be from the tax return side.

I had a situation just this week where an elderly couple came in, and they had a letter from the State of Iowa wanting sales tax monies. Their personal income tax return had a 1099 attached for each of them and the tax return stated they did janitorial work. Neither of these two people could do janitorial work if they had to. They weren't physically capable of doing it. It turns out that the company that's paying them is owned by a family member, and basically what they're doing is helping to support Grandma and Grandpa financially. This is commonly called *phantom income.*

Obviously, this was a tough conversation to have with the state auditor!

While the state is closing the sales tax case against this elderly couple, it's unfortunately open another can of worms for the family member that owns the small business. The business is going to have to prove that the couple is being paid for services actually rendered. The business could be faced with a fraud allegation for deducting payments that they shouldn't have. In addition, the couple could be facing a tough road in regards to any tax credits they may have claimed due to the phantom income.

That provides us a with a perfect segue to discussing a broad overview of payroll taxes.

Here in Iowa, we have both state and federal withholding, along with unemployment taxes, which are paid by the employer. There is no deduction out of the employee's paycheck for any kind of unemployment.

The big thing here, obviously, is making sure that these actually get paid. In Iowa, and I think a lot of states do this, but their main trick to force somebody into compliance is to disallow renewal of various licenses. This includes vehicles licenses and driver's licenses, business licenses, and various professional licenses. This can even occur when somebody is on a payment plan, the state can block somebody from renewing their driver's license. So I can't have my driver's license, which means I can't drive my car which, means I can't get to the job that's going to provide the income that's going to pay the government.

Unfortunately, the state can have an 'I don't care' attitude about this. Obviously the message there is pay them. At least the IRS, if you get behind on payroll taxes, even though the interest and penalties aren't pretty, most of the time you to have a payment plan with them without having any further problems, as long as you stay current.

Let's shift gears back to people that are looking to start a business rather than having an established business. If somebody comes to me and they say, "I've invented a widget and I'm going to open a widget factory," what am I going to advise them on?

The first thing we usually want to talk about, once we get past what the widget is and what their initial plans are, is getting a *business plan* in place. Without that business plan, anything they do going forward is really almost not even worth pursuing because they don't have any checks or balances to keep themselves in line. They need those checks and balances going forward. They need to start thinking about writing a business plan and, within that business plan, lay out how they're going to market their widget and how they're going to manufacture their widget. What are the key numbers that they need to keep track of to make them profitable? If you come to me without a business plan, we're going to spend a lot of time talking about putting one together.

Second, we also need to talk about how you are going to fund this business. Where is the money coming from? What's it going to cost you to do this? What are you going to do with X in the event of Y? Are you going to be able to sustain it? Are you going to be able to go forward, or is this particular event potentially a show stopper for you? We need to plan for these things and know what might be the road block to put you out of business, and be able to address that before it happens. *Contingency planning is key!*

Third, they have to know how to market 'the widget'. How are they going to sell this thing? Who's their customer? How do we bring them into the fold? How do we sell them? What's your message to the market to be able to make everybody think that they need your widget?

Last, but probably most important, get your *team* established. Let's get you an attorney that you are comfortable working with that can set up your legal entity. I'll work with the attorney to help get that entity set up, make sure the paperwork with the Secretary of State is all filed, get your EIN, and other important matters taken care of.

Next, make sure you have your accounting person in place. Whether that's me, your spouse, an employee, a part-time person, get that person in place and trained up on the system that you'll be using. Of course, this also means getting that recordkeeping system in place (see chapter 3). Make sure that, from day one, you are properly tracking your expenditures and your income coming in so that you can react to different things that are going on in the business.

Another person they need is a banker. If there is a situation where they need some money to invest in making the widget a better widget, invest in new technology, etc. They certainly need that banker on board ahead of time. You can't go find somebody at the last minute and expect that they're going to perform in the time frame you need them to perform with, without prior knowledge of you and your business.

When it comes to building your team, remember that none of us operate in a silo. The people that you surround yourself with that are consultants, advisors, the service providers that you turn to in order to outsource certain functions of your business, or that you look to for advice, mentorship, etc., are all very important members of your business team. How you select these advisors is just as important as simply having them.

Selection criteria might be as simple as a referral from somebody. Whether that somebody might be from me, somebody that they know through a friend or a family member. A lot of people don't know an attorney. A lot of people don't know a bookkeeper, or an accountant. The fact that a person is sitting in front of me, for example, if they're brand new to my firm, then most people have gotten here because somebody has told them to be here. They need to be able to establish an open, working relationship with all of those people so that they can pick up the phone and move forward when necessary.

Another very important member of your team is a *mentor*. That mentor doesn't necessarily have to be somebody that knows your business, but rather somebody that you go to and unload the day's problems or successes on, and that person understands you.

Personally, I have a guy that I grew up with. Our grandfathers immigrated together from Italy, and if I have a problem going on in my life or in my day I can pick up the phone almost anytime, and I can scream and yell at him, and he just knows me well enough to understand. He knows how to respond and get me back on track, and vice versa. You need to find that person. Whether it's a friend, whether it's a parent, whether it's a co-worker or a partner. Maybe it's your spouse.

Whoever it is, you need to have somebody that you can turn to in the worst of times just get it all out on the table so that you can pick yourself up and go forward, and conversely you need to be able to go to that person and be able to celebrate your successes.

I also believe that you need to have a business mentor that understands your actual line of business, or your particular type of widget. I think these types or mentors are important along the way to justify in your mind that what you're doing is good. We all have room for improvement, and there are multiple ways to look at any issue or factor in order to help make it better. Having a business coach that understands your industry or widget can make this process infinitely easier.

In the coming chapters, we're going to go into much greater detail on many of these subjects. It is my hope that this first chapter has aligned your thought processes in such a way that you have both an open mind going forward, and a clearer recognition for what you can do yourself, and what you should be open to having other experts do for you.

Chapter 2: Choosing The Right Business Structure

In the last chapter, we briefly discussed the tax situation for self-employed individuals. That discussion applies to small businesses that have chosen not to create a legal entity separate from themselves.

The absolute most simple business structure to set up is the sole proprietorship. The terms self-employed and sole proprietor mean the exact same thing – especially from a tax perspective.

On the federal side, you don't need to do anything special to create a sole proprietorship. As far as the IRS is concerned, as long as you pay those self-employment taxes and file the extra forms required with your personal income tax return, you're in business.

Of course, your state, county, and even city may have additional requirements. The most common requirements are to obtain a local business license and to register a trade name (also known as a DBA – "doing business as").

There are a lot of downsides to operating as a sole proprietor. While beyond the scope of this book, this business type has the greatest liability exposure for the owner. This form of operation also incurs the highest personal tax bill, as we discussed in the last chapter.

A better way to operate is to create a business entity that is legally separate and distinct from yourself as an individual. The most common types of legal entities that you may be familiar with include corporations, partnerships, and the new-fangled LLC (limited liability company).

What this is technically doing is we are now separating your business activity from your own personal self. There are several advantages to creating this sort of separation, including a lot of little things you wouldn't normally consider.

Far and away the two biggest reasons for creating the separate entity, however, are the liability protection and the tax planning benefits.

Let's look at the liability factor. If I offer a delivery service business and I happen to get into an accident, the other person may sue the business. If there is no legal separation between myself and the business, then they are going to be suing me personally. If I have an LLC or corporation, however, they may be limited to just suing the company, providing a layer of protection for myself personally.

The level of risk of your business activity is something you should discuss with an asset protection attorney in order to help determine the best type of business entity for you from this perspective.

Let's talk about the tax side of things. It's pretty common these days to hear people talking about LLCs. This is the most common business entity type to hear about on the radio, TV, and online. The reality is that an LLC isn't for everybody, and it may not be the right type of business entity for you.

More often than not, an LLC is really geared, in my opinion, for either small businesses that won't end up doing much in gross sales or rental properties. In my experience, many businesses are much better off being run as corporations, and they are very similar to an LLC in some regards, but the filing and reporting requirements are a little bit different.

Regardless of whether it's an LLC or a corporation we're talking about, the liability protection is very similar, if done properly. It should also be noted that, while overall audit risk is pretty low either way, your audit is actually lower with an LLC or corporation than it is for a sole proprietorship. This is just one more benefit to setting up the proper entity for your business.

The reason for this is because these business entities are going to have greater reporting requirements than a sole proprietorship. For example, you may be required to report a balance sheet – meaning that you are required to report your assets and debts. This is never required in a sole proprietorship situation.

Due to these enhanced reporting requirements, the IRS

often just assumes that everything is going to be reported correctly. This is especially true because of the assumption that more complicated businesses are going to use the services of a professional accountant, such as myself.

When you operate a separate entity, as already mentioned, you're going to have some more reporting and filing requirements. For an LLC or corporation, you're going to have a separate tax return filed for that particular business. Then, the business is going to issue a form K-1 to you personally for use in filing your personal income tax return. This K-1 is similar to a W-2 or 1099 in some regards, but contains a lot more information and can be much more complicated.

In addition, depending on how your company is structured, you may also be set up as an employee of your own company, and thus receive aW-2.

If you set up an LLC and you are the only owner, the IRS will actually classify you as a self-employed, sole proprietorship. This is because under federal law, there is no specific tax treatment for LLCs.

If you create your LLC with two or more owners (technically called "members"), then you will be classified by the IRS as a partnership by default.

These default classifications are usually not in your best interest. For example, accepting the default classification of sole proprietorship or partnership for an LLC does not eliminate the self-employment tax issue.

At the same time, we want to avoid the double taxation element of having a corporation. The double taxation problem arises because, for regular corporations, the corporate entity itself is required to pay income tax on any profits. Then, when these profits are passed on to the owners (shareholders) in the form of dividends, you have to pay personal income tax on that money *again*.

In order to avoid this, most small businesses will opt to be treated as a *small corporation*, referred to as a "subchapter S corporation" for the section of the law that creates this special tax classification. An S-corporation is a pass through entity, meaning that all profits are passed through directly to the owners, rather than being taxed at the entity level. This entirely eliminates the double taxation problem.

Choosing to be treated as an S-corporation is completely optional. In order to elect to be treated this way, you must file IRS Form 2553. There are specific requirements that need to be met in order to file this form, and it can only be done at certain times of the year.

In my experience, the S-corp structure is the best for the vast majority of small businesses. The nice thing about the S-corp is that just about any entity type can select this election. For example, a single owner LLC, a two owner LLC, a 5 owner LLC, and a corporation can all choose to be treated as an S-corporation.

There are specific rules that all S-corporations must meet. For example, they are not allowed to have more than 25 owners, members, or shareholders. There are additional rules regarding the fiscal year of the business, foreign investors, and more. Please call my office at (515) 986-5843 to schedule an appointment to discuss your particular situation and see if you are eligible to elect S-corp status.

For many single-member LLCs, choosing S-corp status can easily save you up to $15,000 per year, even after taking into account the slight increase in your administrative costs associated with the increased reporting requirements for the S-corp. This one thing might prove to be the best tax planning strategy you every use!

There is one particular requirement of this S-corp strategy that, for some reason, tends to scare some people. Any owners of the S-corp that actively participate in the operation of the business are required to draw some form of paycheck from the business.

The reason for this requirement is simple. As an S-corp, you pay no self-employment taxes on profits that are passed through to you. In fact, you don't pay ANY Social Security and Medicare taxes, period, on any of that pass-through profit. This is actually why we use the S-corp – to save on those exact taxes.

Unfortunately, we can't do this for every dime we take from the company. Part of the same section of law that created this beautiful S-corp benefit was also a requirement that it can't be used to avoid paying all Social Security and Medicare taxes – otherwise nobody would pay them!

The actual money that today's retired seniors paid in to this system their entire life is long gone. All Social Security and Medicare benefits for current recipients is actually paid for by the people that are currently working and paying these taxes. Thus, the IRS is very concerned about the payment and collection of these taxes, because it's what keeps the system going for people currently collecting Social Security benefits.

In order to make sure that all small business owners are paying their fair share into the Social Security and Medicare Trust Funds (these monies are often called "trust fund taxes" by the IRS), everybody at the business is required to be paid *reasonable compensation*, including owners and shareholders.

The definition of what constitutes a "reasonable" paycheck for an S-corp small business owner is one of the most frequently and hotly contested issues every year in tax court. Every year, there are many reasonable compensation cases that go in front of the tax courts, and many more end up in audit situations.

We mentioned earlier that S-corps have lower audit rates than sole proprietorships. The one exception to this, however, is S-corps that don't pay reasonable compensation to their owners. If you want to get audited, this is the fastest way to ensure it happens!

When you pay yourself wages or salary from the business, you pay into Social Security and Medicare. The business still gets to deduct it's half of that money on the corporate return.

So how does this save you money? Let's say your business generates $100,000 in bottom line profit. For what you do, let's say that $50,000 is a "reasonable" salary for yourself. In this example, a self-employed person is going to pay 15.3% self-employment tax on the full $100,000 in profit. The S-corp owner, on the other hand, is only going to pay that tax on the $50,000 in salary. The other $50,000 in profit still requires payment of income tax, but you save that 15.3%. In this example, <u>that's a savings of $7,650 in one year</u>!

So how much salary do you have to take in order to be reasonable, and avoid any risks? This will depend on a LOT of factors, but common things to take into consideration include the salary for somebody in your area doing a similar job, the number of hours you actually work, the responsibilities you take on versus other staff members, and more.

Let's go back to why many business owners don't want to pay themselves a salary (aside from not wanting to pay ANY Social Security taxes!). If you don't currently have any other employees, you're going to need to create a payroll system for just yourself, and this can be quite burdensome.

You're not only going to have to start filing five new tax returns each year to the IRS, but you're also going to have state reporting requirements (unless you live in one of the few states without a state income tax). You're also going to have to make frequent (usually monthly) payments to the IRS and state to pay over those employment taxes.

This extra burden of having a proper payroll process is daunting to most people. Fortunately, an entire industry exists in this country that allows you to outsource this service for a very reasonable fee. Finding the right *payroll processor* to handle all aspects of this for you is quick and painless – and then YOU don't have to worry about it!

Hiring a payroll service for just one employee is very affordable, and worth doing to have it done right. This does eat into the tax savings, of course, but you still come out ahead. Paying a few hundred dollars per year for a payroll service is more than worth being able to save THOUSANDS on your tax bill.

Please call my office directly at (515) 986-5843 to discuss how an S-Corp can save you money, and to discuss setting up your payroll processing.

Chapter 3: Keeping The Books

One of the number one things that gets small business owners into trouble is that they lack a proper recordkeeping system.

In this chapter, we're going to take a look at what kinds of records you should be keeping, why you must keep records, and how to best keep those records. We'll also talk about how long you need to keep certain records for tax purposes

Why do I need to keep books?

Everybody that runs a business, from the smallest home office to the largest multi-national corporation, but maintain certain accounting and financial records. With good records, you'll be able to do accomplish many things, such as the following.

Monitor the progress of your business. You need good records to monitor the progress of your business. Records can show whether your business is improving, which items are selling, or what changes you need to make. Good records can increase the likelihood of business success.

Prepare your financial statements. You need good records to prepare accurate financial statements. These include income (profit and loss) statements and balance sheets. These statements can help you in dealing with your bank or creditors and help you manage your business.

- An income statement shows the income and expenses of the business for a given period of time.
- A balance sheet shows the assets, liabilities, and your equity in the business on a given date.

Identify source of receipts.   You will receive money or property from many sources. Your records can identify the source of your receipts. You need this information to separate business from nonbusiness receipts and taxable from nontaxable income. After all, you don't want to pay tax on things you don't have to!

Keep track of deductible expenses.   The vast majority of the expenses that you incur in the course of operating your business are deductible for tax purposes. A good recordkeeping system will help you capture these expenses when they incur, and save you money on taxes in the long run. You may forget expenses when you prepare your tax return unless you record them when they occur.

Prepare your tax returns.   You need good records to prepare your tax returns. These records must support the income, expenses, and credits you report. Generally, these are the same records you use to monitor your business and prepare your financial statements.

Support items reported on tax returns.   You must keep your business records available at all times for inspection by the IRS and state tax authorities. If the

IRS examines any of your tax returns, you may be asked to explain the items reported. A complete set of records will not only speed up the process, but also ensure that you are not denied any tax benefits to which you are fully entitled.

What kinds of records do I need to keep?

Contrary to popular belief, the law does not require any specific recordkeeping system for your business unless you are publicly seeking investors or offering various types of investments. In other words, you can choose any recordkeeping system suited to your business, as long as it allows you to meet tax reporting obligations.

The business you are in affects the type of records you need to keep for federal tax purposes. You should set up your recordkeeping system using an accounting method that clearly shows your income for your tax year. You should consult with a competent professional for assistance in choosing the accounting method that's right for you.

In the event that you operate multiple businesses, each business needs to have a unique and separate set of records. It is particularly important to keep income and expenses assigned to the right business, and even more important to keep personal expenses separate from business expenses.

In addition, a corporation should keep minutes of board of directors' meetings, even if the only board member is yourself.

Your recordkeeping system should include a summary of your business transactions. This summary is ordinarily made in your bookkeeping system. This system should include your total income, as well as expenses that you are deducting. For most small businesses, the business checkbook or bank statement is the main source for entries in the business books. In addition, you must keep supporting documents, explained later.

What about electronic records? More and more businesses these days are choosing to do ALL their recordkeeping electronically. All requirements that apply to hard copy books and records also apply to electronic storage systems that maintain tax records. When you upgrade from physical records to electronic, you must keep the electronic data for just as long as you need to keep paper copies.

The primary requirement for any electronic recordkeeping system is that the system must be able to display information in a human-readable format. In other words, me, you, and the IRS all need to be able to read what's stored and understand it. If requested by a government regulator, such as the IRS, the electronic system must be able to display records in such a way as to validate whatever it is you're trying to support.

As technology brings us more and more options for recordkeeping, some small business become fearful of migrating 100% to these new systems. However, these systems are not only easier to use, but they also tend to actually be far more affordable than keeping years and years of business records in storage. Once converted to electronic format, the original can actually be safely destroyed. If you would like assistance in switching to a modern electronic system, please give my office a call.

What about supporting documents?

In the normal course of conducting business, you're going to generate a lot of supporting documents. The information from these documents needs to be recorded in your recordkeeping system. These documents might include:

- sales slips
- paid bills
- invoices
- receipts
- deposit slips
- canceled checks

It is important to keep these documents because they support the entries in your books and on your tax return. Keep them in an orderly fashion and in a safe place. For instance, organize them by year and type of income or expense. As mentioned earlier, it is perfectly acceptable to keep these documents in an electronic format.

Let's Talk The Talk, So We Can Walk The Walk

In the course of running your business, you're going to encounter many accounting terms that it can be helpful to have a basic understanding of. Being able to speak the common "language" of business will come in handy when speaking with suppliers, vendors, customers, tax authorities, business managers, consultants, and many other professionals that you'll interact with.

Gross receipts.   Gross receipts are the income you receive from your business. You should keep supporting documents that show the amounts and sources of your gross receipts. Documents that show gross receipts include the following.

- Cash register tapes.
- Bank deposit slips.
- Receipt books.
- Invoices.
- Credit card charge slips.
- Forms 1099-MISC.

Inventory.   Inventory is any item you buy and resell to customers. If you are a manufacturer or producer, this includes the cost of all raw materials or parts purchased for manufacture into finished products. Your supporting documents should show the amount paid and that the amount was for inventory. Documents reporting the cost of inventory include the following.

- Canceled checks.
- Cash register tape receipts.
- Credit card sales slips.
- Invoices.

These records will help you determine the value of your inventory at the end of the year. Valuing inventory is an important process for tax purposes, and should be discussed with your accounting professional.

Expenses.   Expenses are the costs you incur (other than the cost of inventory) to carry on your business. Your supporting documents should show the amount paid and that the amount was for a business expense. Documents for expenses include the following.

- Canceled checks.
- Cash register tapes.
- Account statements.
- Credit card sales slips.
- Invoices.
- Petty cash slips for small cash payments.

A petty cash fund allows you to make small payments without having to write checks for small amounts. Each time you make a payment from this fund, you should make out a petty cash slip and attach it to your receipt as proof of payment.

Travel, transportation, entertainment, and gift expenses. The rules and recordkeeping requirements pertaining to these particular expenses would take up an entire book of their own. It is very important that detailed records regarding the exact business purpose of these expenses be maintained. In particular, the IRS will require detailed written mileage logs to support this particular deduction. Be sure to keep a mileage log in each vehicle you use for business purposes, and be sure to actually use it. Speak with your tax professional for additional assistance with maintaining these records.

Payroll. This is another major enforcement area for the IRS and the state. Not only do you have to be concerned with wage and hour laws, but you must also pay employment taxes at specific times. The failure to pay these payroll taxes is a very major offense, and could lead to significant personal liability for the unpaid taxes. Due to the complex nature of payroll, it is highly recommended that you work with a professional on this one!

Assets. Assets are the property, such as machinery and furniture you own and use in your business. You must keep records to verify certain information about your business assets. You need records to figure the annual depreciation and the gain or loss when you sell the assets. Your records should show the following information.

- When and how you acquired the asset.
- Purchase price.
- Cost of any improvements.
- Section 179 deduction taken.
- Deductions taken for depreciation.
- Deductions taken for casualty losses, such as losses resulting from fires or storms.
- How you used the asset.
- When and how you disposed of the asset.
- Selling price.
- Expenses of sale.

The following documents may show this information.

- Purchase and sales invoices.
- Real estate closing statements.
- Canceled checks.

What if I don't have a canceled check?   If you do not have a canceled check, you may be able to prove payment with certain financial account statements prepared by financial institutions. These include account statements prepared for the financial institution by a third party. These account statements must be highly legible. The following table lists acceptable account statements.

IF payment is by...	THEN the statement must show the...
Check	<ul><li>Check number.</li><li>Amount.</li><li>Payee's name.</li><li>Date the check amount was posted to the account by the financial institution.</li></ul>
Electronic funds transfer	<ul><li>Amount transferred.</li><li>Payee's name.</li><li>Date the transfer was posted to the account by the financial institution.</li></ul>
Credit card	<ul><li>Amount charged.</li><li>Payee's name.</li><li>Transaction date.</li></ul>

Proof of payment of an amount, by itself, does not establish you are entitled to a tax deduction. For example, the details on a credit card statement alone are not proof of the business purpose for an expense. You should also keep other documents, such as receipts and invoices, to show that you also incurred the cost and that it was a legitimate business expense.

Recording Business Transactions

A good recordkeeping system includes a summary of your business transactions. Business transactions are ordinarily summarized in books called *journals* and *ledgers*. You can buy them at your local stationery or office supply store, or use bookkeeping software instead.

A *journal* is a book where you record each business transaction shown on your supporting documents. You may have to keep separate journals for transactions that occur frequently.

A *ledger* is a book that contains the totals from all of your journals. It is organized into different *accounts*. If you use a bookkeeping software system, it will replicate these exact same items.

Whether you keep journals and ledgers and how you keep them depends on the type of business you are in. For example, a recordkeeping system for a small business might include the following items.

- Business checkbook.
- Daily summary of cash receipts.
- Monthly summary of cash receipts.
- Check disbursements journal.
- Depreciation worksheet.
- Employee compensation record.

The system you use to record business transactions will be more effective if you follow good recordkeeping practices. For example, record expenses when they occur, and identify the source of recorded receipts. Generally, it is best to record transactions on a daily basis.

Business checkbook. One of the first things you should do when you start a business is open a business checking account at a bank. You should keep your business account separate from your personal checking account in order to avoid confusion and issues with *commingling*.

The business checkbook is your basic source of information for recording your business expenses. You should deposit all daily receipts in your business checking account. You should check your account for errors by reconciling it.

Consider using a checkbook that allows enough space to identify the source of deposits as business income, personal funds, or loans. You should also note on the deposit slip the source of the deposit and keep copies of all slips.

You should make all payments by check to document business expenses. Write checks payable to yourself only when making withdrawals from your business for personal use. Avoid writing checks payable to cash. If you must write a check for cash to pay a business expense, include the receipt for the cash payment in your records. If you cannot get a receipt for a cash payment, you should make an adequate explanation in your records at the time of payment.

Use the business account for business purposes only. Indicate the source of deposits and the type of expense in the checkbook.

Reconciling the checking account.   When you receive your bank statement, make sure the statement, your checkbook, and your books agree. The statement balance may not agree with the balance in your checkbook and books if the statement:

- Includes bank charges you did not enter in your books and subtract from your checkbook balance, or
- Does not include deposits made after the statement date or checks that did not clear your account before the statement date.

By reconciling your checking account, you will:

- Verify how much money you have in the account,
- Make sure that your checkbook and books reflect all bank charges and the correct balance in the checking account, and
- Correct any errors in your bank statement, checkbook, and books.

You should reconcile your checking account each month.

Before you reconcile your monthly bank statement, check your own figures. Begin with the balance shown in your checkbook at the end of the previous month. To this balance, add the total cash deposited during the month and subtract the total cash disbursements.

After checking your figures, the result should agree with your checkbook balance at the end of the month. If the result does not agree, you may have made an error in recording a check or deposit. You can find the error by doing the following.

1. Adding the amounts on your check stubs and comparing that total with the total in the "amount of check" column in your check disbursements journal. If the totals do not agree, check the individual amounts to see if an error was made in your check stub record or in the related entry in your check disbursements journal.
2. Adding the deposit amounts in your checkbook. Compare that total with the monthly total in your cash receipt book, if you have one. If the totals do not agree, check the individual amounts to find any errors.

If your checkbook and journal entries still disagree, then refigure the running balance in your checkbook to make sure additions and subtractions are correct.

When your checkbook balance agrees with the balance figured from the journal entries, you may begin reconciling your checkbook with the bank statement. Many banks print a reconciliation worksheet on the back of the statement.

To reconcile your account, follow these steps.

1. Compare the deposits listed on the bank statement with the deposits shown in your checkbook. Note all differences in the dollar amounts.
2. Compare each canceled check, including both check number and dollar amount, with the entry in your checkbook. Note all differences in the dollar amounts. Mark the check number in the checkbook as having cleared the bank. After accounting for all checks returned by the bank, those not marked in your checkbook are your outstanding checks.
3. Prepare a bank reconciliation.
4. Update your checkbook and journals for items shown on the reconciliation as not recorded (such as service charges) or recorded incorrectly.

At this point, the adjusted bank statement balance should equal your adjusted checkbook balance. If you still have differences, check the previous steps to find the errors.

Types of Bookkeeping Systems

There are two general types of bookkeeping systems that you can choose from: Single-entry and double-entry. You must decide whether to use a single-entry or a double-entry bookkeeping system. The single-entry system of bookkeeping is the simplest to maintain, but it may not be suitable for everyone. You may find the double-entry system better because it has built-in checks and balances to assure accuracy and control.

Single-entry.   A single-entry system is based on the income statement (profit or loss statement). It can be a simple and practical system if you are starting a small business. The system records the flow of income and expenses through the use of:

1.   A daily summary of cash receipts, and
2.   Monthly summaries of cash receipts and disbursements.

Double-entry.   A double-entry bookkeeping system uses journals and ledgers. Transactions are first entered in a journal and then posted to ledger accounts. These accounts show income, expenses, assets (property a business owns), liabilities (debts of a business), and net worth (excess of assets over liabilities). You close income and expense accounts at the end of each tax year. You keep asset, liability, and net worth accounts open on a permanent basis.

In the double-entry system, each account has a left side for debits and a right side for credits. It is self-balancing because you record every transaction as a debit entry in one account and as a credit entry in another.

Under this system, the total debits must equal the total credits after you post the journal entries to the ledger accounts. If the amounts do not balance, you have made an error and you must find and correct it.

An example of a journal entry exhibiting a payment of rent in October is shown next.

Computerized System

There are computer software packages you can use for recordkeeping. They can be purchased in many retail stores. These packages are very helpful and relatively easy to use; they require very little knowledge of bookkeeping and accounting. The new era of cloud-based bookkeeping systems are even easier to use, and most of them can import transactions directly from your bank and credit card issuers via their online banking systems.

If you use a computerized system, you must be able to produce sufficient legible records to support and verify entries made on your return and determine your correct tax liability. To meet this qualification, the machine-sensible records must reconcile with your books and return. These records must provide enough detail to identify the underlying source documents.

You must also keep all machine-sensible records and a complete description of the computerized portion of your recordkeeping system. This documentation must be sufficiently detailed to show all of the following items.

- Functions being performed as the data flows through the system.
- Controls used to ensure accurate and reliable processing.
- Controls used to prevent the unauthorized addition, alteration, or deletion of retained records.
- Charts of accounts and detailed account descriptions.

How Long To Keep Records

You must keep your records as long as they may be needed for the administration of any provision of the Internal Revenue Code. Generally, this means you must keep records that support an item of income or deduction on a return until the period of limitations for that return runs out.

The period of limitations is the period of time in which you can amend your return to claim a credit or refund, or the IRS can assess additional tax. Table 1 contains the periods of limitations that apply to income tax returns. Unless otherwise stated, the years refer to the period after the return was filed. Returns filed before the due date are treated as filed on the due date.

Keep copies of your filed tax returns. They help in preparing future tax returns and making computations if you file an amended return.

Employment taxes.   If you have employees, you must keep all employment tax records for at least 4 years after the date the tax becomes due or is paid, whichever is later. For more information about recordkeeping for employment taxes, see Publication 15.

Assets.   Keep records relating to property until the period of limitations expires for the year in which you dispose of the property in a taxable disposition. You must keep these records to figure any depreciation, amortization, or depletion deduction, and to figure your basis for computing gain or loss when you sell or otherwise dispose of the property.

  Generally, if you received property in a nontaxable exchange, your basis in that property is the same as the basis of the property you gave up, increased by any money you paid. You must keep the records on the old property, as well as on the new property, until the period of limitations expires for the year in which you dispose of the new property in a taxable disposition.

Records for nontax purposes.   When your records are no longer needed for tax purposes, do not discard them until you check to see if you have to keep them longer for other purposes. For example, your insurance company or creditors may require you to keep them longer than the IRS does.

Table 1. Period of Limitations

IF you...	THEN the period is...
1. Owe additional tax and situations (2), (3), and (4), below, do not apply to you	3 years
2. Do not report income that you should report and it is more than 25% of the gross income shown on the return	6 years
3. File a fraudulent return	Not limited
4. Do not file a return	Not limited
5. File a claim for credit or refund after you filed your return	Later of: 3 years or 2 years after tax was paid
6. File a claim for a loss from worthless securities or a bad debt deduction	7 years

Deducting Business Expenses

You can deduct business expenses on your business or personal income tax return, depending on the form of your business. These are the current operating costs of running your business. To be deductible, a business expense must be both ordinary and necessary. An ordinary expense is one that is common and accepted in your field of business, trade, or profession. A necessary expense is one that is helpful and appropriate for your business, trade, or profession. An expense does not have to be indispensable to be considered necessary.

The following are brief explanations of some expenses that are of interest to people starting a business. There are many other expenses that you may be able to deduct.

Business Start-Up Costs

Business start-up costs are the expenses you incur before you actually begin business operations. Your business start-up costs will depend on the type of business you are starting. They may include costs for advertising, travel, surveys, and training. These costs are generally capital expenses.

You usually recover costs for a particular asset (such as machinery or office equipment) through depreciation (discussed next). You can elect to deduct up to $5,000 of business start-up costs and $5,000 of organizational costs paid or incurred after October 22, 2004. The $5,000 deduction is reduced by the amount your total start-up or organizational costs exceed $50,000. Any remaining cost must be amortized.

Depreciation

If property you acquire to use in your business has a useful life that extends substantially beyond the year it is placed in service, you generally cannot deduct the entire cost as a business expense in the year you acquire it. You must spread the cost over more than one tax year and deduct part of it each year. This method of deducting the cost of business property is called depreciation.

Business property you must depreciate includes the following items.

- Office furniture.
- Buildings.
- Machinery and equipment.

You can choose to deduct a limited amount of the cost of certain depreciable property in the year you place the property in service. This deduction is known as the "section 179 deduction."

Depreciation must be taken in the year it is allowable. Allowable depreciation not taken in a prior year cannot be taken in the current year. If you do not deduct the correct depreciation, you may be able to make a correction by filing Form 1040X, Amended U.S. Individual Income Tax Return, or by changing your accounting method.

Business Use of Your Home

To deduct expenses related to the business use of part of your home, you must meet specific requirements. Even then, your deduction may be limited. You may be able to use the simplified method to figure your expenses for business use of your home. For more information, see Schedule C (Form 1040) and its instructions.

To qualify to claim expenses for business use of your home, you must meet both the following tests.

1. Your use of the business part of your home must be:
   a. Exclusive,
   b. Regular,
   c. For your trade or business, AND
2. The business part of your home must be one of the following:
   a. Your principal place of business (defined later),
   b. A place where you meet or deal with patients, clients, or customers in the normal course of your trade or business, or
   c. A separate structure (not attached to your home) you use in connection with your trade or business.

Exclusive use.   To qualify under the exclusive use test, you must use a specific area of your home only for your trade or business. The area used for business can be a room or other separately identifiable space. The space does not need to be marked off by a permanent partition.

You do not meet the requirements of the exclusive use test if you use the area in question both for business and for personal purposes.

Exceptions to exclusive use.   You do not have to meet the exclusive use test if either of the following applies.

1. You use part of your home for the storage of inventory or product samples.
2. You use part of your home as a daycare facility.

Principal place of business.   Your home office will qualify as your principal place of business for deducting expenses for its use if you meet the following requirements.

- You use it exclusively and regularly for administrative or management activities of your trade or business.
- You have no other fixed location where you conduct substantial administrative or management activities of your trade or business.

Alternatively, if you use your home exclusively and regularly for your business, but your home office does not qualify as your principal place of business based on the previous rules, you determine your principal place of business based on the following factors.

- The relative importance of the activities performed at each location.
- If the relative importance factor does not determine your principal place of business, the time spent at each location.

If, after considering your business locations, your home cannot be identified as your principal place of business, you cannot deduct home office expenses.

Vehicle Expenses

If you use your car or truck in your business, you can deduct the costs of operating and maintaining it. You generally can deduct either your actual expenses or the standard mileage rate.

Actual expenses. If you deduct actual expenses, you can deduct the cost of the following items:

- Depreciation
- Registration/Tags
- Parking space/garage rent
- Tolls
- Insurance
- Licenses

- Repairs
- Gas
- Oil

If you use your vehicle for both business and personal purposes, you must divide your expenses between business and personal use. You can divide your expenses based on the miles driven for each purpose.

Standard mileage rate.   Instead of figuring actual expenses, you may be able to use the standard mileage rate to figure the deductible costs of operating your car, van, pickup, or panel truck for business purposes. You can use the standard mileage rate for a vehicle you own or lease. The standard mileage rate is a specified amount of money you can deduct for each business mile you drive. It is announced annually by the IRS. To figure your deduction, multiply your business miles by the standard mileage rate for the year.

Generally, if you use the standard mileage rate, you cannot deduct your actual expenses. However, you may be able to deduct business-related parking fees, tolls, interest on your car loan, and certain state and local taxes.

Choosing the standard mileage rate.   If you want to use the standard mileage rate for a car you own, you must choose to use it in the first year the car is available to your business. In later years, you can choose to use either the standard mileage rate or actual expenses.

<u>Bottom line: Don't be shy, claim EVERY tax benefit you're legally entitled to!</u> Give me a call at (515) 986-5843 to schedule a review of your tax returns for potentially missed tax benefits.

Jim McClaflin, EA

Chapter 4: Nasty Things The IRS Can Do To You That You Never Want To Experience

A Notice of Federal Tax Lien (NFTL) is an encumbrance that establishes a legal claim by the government. It does <u>not</u> result in the physical seizure of your property. A levy, on the other hand, allows the IRS to actually seize wages, cash, or property. Levies are normally divided into two categories. The first category includes tangible, real and personal property that you own. The second category includes third parties who hold property belonging to you such as bank deposits and wages.

The first category is often referred to as a "seizure", while the second category is usually referred to as a "levy" or "garnishment". The IRS must file a lien before they can issue a levy and must place a levy upon your property before they can seize your property. Levy action is the usually the most severe collections action the IRS takes against the majority of people that owe back taxes, and it is this type of action that an IRS employee is referring to when they talk about **"enforced collection."**

Federal Tax Liens

Once the IRS makes a valid assessment against you, the IRS is required to give notice and demand for payment within 60 days by law. If you don't pay the taxes owed, a Federal Tax Lien automatically arises and attaches to property and property rights either own directly by you or acquired after the date of the tax assessment.

Both Federal law and state law are relevant in determining the effect of the Federal Tax Lien against you and your property. Federal laws determine whether the tax lien has validly attached and state law aids in determining to what property the lien attaches. Under your state laws certain property may be exempt from the lien.

In general, a tax lien gives the IRS a claim against everything you own, from your home and car all the way to the rusted bicycle in your backyard. The lien also technically attaches to your wages, money in you bank accounts, your retirement accounts, and even the cash in your wallet.

A Federal Tax Lien also impacts your credit score, since it shows up on your credit report. Therefore, the tax lien can impact your ability to obtain loans, rent an apartment, and can even impact your insurance rates and ability to obtain employment if you are a job seeker.

In most cases, a tax lien will jump ahead of many other liens against your property after a 180 day period, unless a particular piece of property is used as collateral for a loan. For example, a tax lien does not jump ahead in priority position over a car loan or a first, second, or third mortgage against your home. It will, however, usually jump ahead of, say, a mechanic's lien against your home.

You may have circumstances where having the lien released would be of benefit to helping you resolve the tax situation. There are three types of lien releases available to a taxpayer that may help you resolve tax liabilities with the IRS.

Certificate of Discharge

A Certificate of Discharge (COD) is the process of removing a single piece of property from being subject to the tax lien, usually so that the property can be legally transferred. For example, if you are trying to sell your house but the presence of the lien is preventing this from occurring, then you would need to obtain a Certificate of Discharge to release the tax lien against your house.

In the vast majority of cases, the IRS will not release a lien against a particular piece of property unless they are somehow going to benefit from it. They will generally approve a Certificate of Discharge if the lien discharge will facilitate the sale of the property in such a way that the IRS will get some money out of it. In other words, releasing the lien will facilitate collection of the tax.

If the government isn't going to see any money out of releasing a piece of property from the lien, it's possible to still obtain a Certificate of Discharge if there is a valid reason. In particular, if the IRS won't be receiving any money, but getting rid of the property will free up cash flow and put you in a better financial position in regards to your income and expenses so that later on down the road you can start paying on your taxes, then the IRS will likely approve a Certificate of Discharge.

If the property in question has no significant fair market value, the COD may also be granted, but this is much more of a hit-or-miss situation.

Lien Subordination

A lien subordination is the process of moving the tax lien down a notch in the prioritization of claims against a piece of property. For example, if you own a house free and clear, and the tax lien is in first position against the house, you can't obtain a mortgage against the house. No lender in their right mind is going to loan you money against that house unless their lien is going to take first position.

The answer to this problem is the lien subordination. The IRS will usually approve the subordination of their lien against a property if the lien that will be taking first position ahead of the tax lien will result in money going to your tax liability.

In the house example, obtaining a subordination of the tax lien in order to obtain a mortgage against the house will result in cash coming from that mortgage. At closing, that cash will go directly to the IRS, the mortgage will move into first position, and the tax lien gets re-recorded in second position.

Remember, paying interest on a loan is almost always going to be cheaper than paying penalties and interest to the IRS.

There are other conditions where a lien subordination will still be approved, even if the IRS isn't going to obtain direct proceeds from doing so. For example, many trucking companies will finance their accounts receivable through a process called factoring. In factoring, a lender pays the trucking company some percentage of their accounts receivable (usually 75% to 90%) up front, and then the lender takes the responsibility of collecting on that account receivable when it's due, usually 30 to 90 days down the road. This way, the trucking company gets money now so that they can buy fuel and make payroll.

When a tax lien is filed, most factoring lenders stop funding. In that case, the trucking company suddenly loses all it's cash flow. In order to enable the funding to continue, a lien subordination can be obtained that move the tax lien to a position below the factoring lender, thereby protecting the lender's claim on those accounts receivable.

Lien Withdrawal

There are rare occasions when obtaining an outright release of the entire Federal tax lien is actually the best way to progress towards a resolution of your tax liabilities. If a case can be made that the withdrawal of the lien will facilitate payment of the tax liability, or is otherwise in the best interest of both the taxpayer and the government, then the government may be open to this.

Another case where a lien withdrawal can be applied for is when you have entered into an Installment Agreement to pay the back taxes and the agreement did not mandate that a lien be filed, particularly a payment plan where the payments are directly withdrawn from your bank account. In these cases, you can often get the lien released as long as you are current with your payments and other tax obligations.

Certificate of Release of Paid or Unenforceable Lien

The IRS is required to issue a certificate of release of lien no later than 30 days after one of the following events occur:

- The tax liability is paid in full.

- The tax liability is no longer collectible. In other words, the 10-year statute of limitations on collections has expired.

- The IRS accepts the bond of a surety company or payment of all taxes owed is to be made no later than six months before the expiration of the 10-year collection statute.

- The taxpayer delivers a cashier's check to the IRS and receives a Certificate of Release of Tax Lien.

Bank Account Levies

An IRS levy is the actual action taken by the IRS to collect past due taxes. For example, the IRS can issue a bank levy to obtain your cash in savings and checking accounts or the IRS can levy your wages or accounts receivable, if you run a business.

The person, company or institution that is served the levy must comply or face their own IRS problems. For example, when the IRS issues a levy against your bank accounts, your bank must comply. The bank is required to take the funds out of your account to which the levy attaches on the day they process the levy. They must then hold those funds for 21 days and then after the 21 days, send those funds to the IRS. If they fail to do this, the IRS will come after your bank and penalize them. The additional paperwork that the bank or other company or institution is faced with to comply with the levy usually causes your relationship to suffer with the person or institution being levied.

When a financial institution receives a levy on your bank account, it cannot surrender the money until 21 calendar days after the levy has been served. This 21-day waiting period provides you the opportunity to notify the IRS and correct any errors regarding your accounts.

An extension of this 21-day period may be granted by the Area Director of the IRS if there is a legitimate dispute regarding the amount of tax owed. Anytime during the 21-day waiting period the levy can be released. During these 21 days it is imperative that you exercise your appeals rights. In this case, you will want to file a CAP appeal. CAP stands for Collection Appeals Process. When you file a CAP appeal, the IRS must hear your case within five days. Please see the chapter on Appeals for more information about this process.

Levies should be avoided at all costs and are usually the result of poor communication with your Revenue Officer. When the IRS levies a bank account, the levy is only for the particular day the levy is received by the bank. As I mentioned, the bank is required to remove whatever amount of money is available in your account that day up to the maximum amount of the IRS levy and send it to the IRS after that 21 day hold period. This type of levy does not affect future deposits. So if your bank account gets levied today and all the money is taken out by the bank to be sent to the IRS 21 days later, you can make a deposit tomorrow that is not subject to that IRS levy.

An IRS wage levy is quite different. Wage levies are filed with your employer and remain in effect until the IRS notifies the employer that the wage levy has been released. Most wage levies take so much money from your paycheck that you don't have enough money to live on. In most circumstances, an IRS wage garnishment will take 70% to 80% of your entire paycheck. For most taxpayers, wage garnishments are the worst thing the IRS can do to them, and everything possible should be done to avoid this debilitating attack on your personal finances.

Personal Property Levies

The IRS's levy power is extremely broad and does not require that the IRS take you to court. The IRS can use its authority to gain possession of your property to pay any back taxes owed and all they have to do is file a notice in demand of payment, wait 10 days, then file a 30-day notice of intent to levy. After that 30 days, they can then levy. The effect of a levy is to compel you to turn property over to the IRS. Amounts that the IRS gains from a levy or garnishment are applied to your tax debt as follows:

1. The proceeds are applied to the expenses of the levy in sale.

2. Proceeds from the levy are then applied to the tax specifically relating to the levied property.

3. Proceeds are then applied to the delinquent tax liability that caused the whole situation in the first place.

4. Funds collected by a levy are considered to have been paid involuntarily. Therefore, you cannot specify to the IRS how you want those funds applied, which you are normally able to do if you make voluntary payments. This is yet another reason why levies are best avoided.

As we already mentioned, the IRS is required to notify you of its intent to levy you at least 30 days before the levy. This is done thru a notice called a Letter 1058 and states across the top of the notice, "Final Notice of Intent to Levy". When you are issued a Letter 1058 by the IRS, you have broad appeals right that allows you to appeal the proposed action. However, your appeal must be submitted within the 30 day window. If you've recently receive a final notice of intent to levy, please see the Chapter on Appeals to learn how to file a Collection Due Process appeal.

Seizures

The IRS must issue a notice of seizure to the owner of any real property (e.g. real estate) or the possessor of personal property as soon as practicable after the property is seized. This notice has the same effect as the Notice of Levy and can be delivered in person to the owner or possessor of the property or left at your home or normal place of business. Seizures must always be approved by upper IRS management. The supervisor must review your information, verify that the balance is due and affirm that a lien, levy or seizure is appropriate under the circumstances. Failure to give the proper notice will invalidate the seizure and afford you certain legal rights.

Seizures of your residence or business

The IRS is no longer really in the business of seizing homes and entire businesses. These sorts of seizures have become relatively infrequent, largely in due to the adverse publicity that the IRS has received from conducting these actions. The Taxpayer Bill of Rights prohibits the IRS from seizing real property that is used as a residence by the taxpayer for tax amounts of $5,000 or less, including penalties and interest. The Taxpayer Bill of Rights also only permits a levy or seizure on a principal residence if a judge approves of the seizure in writing. Following the 1998 Restructuring Amendments to the Internal Revenue Code, the process for seizing your home has become incredibly difficult for the IRS, which is a good thing for you.

Wage Garnishments

The IRS wage garnishment is a very powerful tool used to collect taxes owed by bringing your employer into the situation. A wage garnishment cannot only be an inconvenience and an embarrassment but it can also leave you with no money to pay your regular living expenses. Once a wage garnishment is filed with your employer, the employer is required to collect the vast majority of each of your paychecks and send that money to the IRS. As mentioned earlier, the wage garnishment will usually take 70% to 80% of your paycheck. In addition, if you receive Social Security, the IRS can take up to 15% of each and every one of your Social Security checks. The wage garnishment stays in effect until either the IRS is paid or the IRS agrees to release the garnishment.

A wage garnishment can be appealed through the Collection Appeals Program, just like a bank account levy. In addition, wage garnishments are a situation where seeking assistance from the Taxpayer Advocate can be extremely helpful.

Fair Debt Collection Practices Act

The IRS is subject to the conditions of the Fair Debt Collection Practices Act just like any other debt collector. This Act includes a number of rules controlling debt collection practices.

For example, you cannot be contacted by a Collections Representative of the IRS outside of the hours of 8AM to 9PM, and it also prohibits harassing or abusive behavior from the IRS to you. The IRS may not communicate with you at an unusual time or place which is known or which should be known to be inconvenient to you. The IRS can also not communicate with you regarding your tax liability at your place of employment if the IRS knows or has reason to know that the your employer prohibits you from receiving such communication.

If the IRS knows that you are represented by someone who is authorized to practice before the IRS, then they can also not contact you. This provision does not apply if your power of attorney representative does not respond to the IRS within a reasonable period of time after being requested to do so. That is why it's important that if you hire professional tax resolution representation that you hire a reputable firm that's going to actually do what you pay them to do.

Jim McClaflin, EA

Chapter 5: Of Time & Taxes

Statutes of limitations in regards to tax matters are important for you to understand because the different statutes of limitations give you different rights and responsibilities in regards to the tax matters involved. There are some statutes of limitations that work for you and there are others that can obviously work against you. It is important for you to understand these statutes of limitations when dealing with the Internal Revenue Service so that you aren't chasing a ghost or trying to make a case that can't be made.

From the government's perspective, the statute of limitations restricts your rights in many ways, such as the restriction on claiming a refund of tax you overpaid or limiting initial actions to obtain refunds.

Now, a statute of limitations may also restrict what the IRS can do against you. The statute of limitations restricts them from collecting a deficiency in tax after a certain amount of time, and also prevents the IRS from asserting either civil or criminal cases.

Either way you look at it, the statute of limitations issue provides a date of finality after which actions may not be taken by either the IRS or by you which is why it is essential for you to understand them.

Let's first look at the three-year rules. First, the IRS must assess a tax within three years after the date that you file a tax return. This three-year period also applies to penalties. Now, when is a tax return considered filed for the purposes of this rule? A return is treated as being filed on time even if it's received by the IRS after the return's due date.

Timely filing is determined by the postmark stamped on the envelope by the U.S. Postal Service or by a private delivery service. That is why whenever you send a tax return or other important items such as an Installment Agreement proposal or an Offer in Compromise application, or an Appeal, I highly recommend that you always send it by certified mail with return receipt requested.

There does not appear to be a "bright line" test to determine whether a tax return lacking a required form is a valid return. Courts will typically apply the "substantial compliance standard" to the facts of each case. This means that there must be adequate information on the return to calculate the tax liability even if a required form was omitted. The document must also indicate that it is, in fact, a tax return. An honest and reasonable attempt must be made to satisfy the tax law and you must execute the return under penalties of perjury, which is what you're doing whenever you sign the bottom of a tax return. Next time you have a tax return in front of you, take a look at what you're actually signing.

A complete tax return that lacks a specific required form such as a schedule or attachment is still sufficient to begin the statute of limitations running for assessment purposes. So for example, if you file your 1040 personal income tax return but you forget to include a Schedule E. Your income from that Schedule E is on the front page of the Form 1040. The IRS can't say that you didn't file a timely return and therefore they have to start the clock ticking on the statute of limitations for the assessment of the tax as soon as they get it.

There are special statute of limitations rules that you need to be aware of as well. When the IRS produces a Substitute for Return – which is prepared by the IRS when you don't file the tax return – this does not start running the statute of limitations for assessment.

In order to start the clock running on the 3-year assessment statute of limitations, you have to file a proper tax return yourself. So, if you have been notified by the IRS that they prepared the return on your behalf, it is generally advisable to file a n actual, original return as soon as possible.

A six-year statute of limitations, instead of three years, applies to returns that omit a substantial amount of income. "Substantial" means an amount of income which exceeds 25% of the gross income reported on the original tax return. The limitations period is extended to the tax payer's entire tax liability for that year, not just the omitted items.

This applies only to innocent or negligent omissions of gross income. The six-year limitations period does not apply to fraudulent omissions of gross income. If you fraudulently omit reporting income on a tax return, the tax may be assessed at any time.

Here's a bonus tip for you: The burden of proof rests with the IRS in proving that the 25% omission from income did in fact occur. The IRS cannot solely rely on the amount of unreported income asserted in the Notice of Deficiency they mail you, which they're required to send you by law

The Internal Revenue Code states that the IRS can assess tax or bring a suit to collect an unassessed tax at any time regardless of any statute of limitations for some specific situations. Here are those situations:

1. You fail to file the tax return.

2. A false or fraudulent return is filed with the intent to evade the tax.

3. The tax payer attempts to defeat or evade the tax.

4. Once the tax payer files a fraudulent return, the tax payer cannot later start the running of the

three-year statute of limitations period by filing an amended return to include the omitted income.

Next, let's talk about statute of limitations on collection of a tax. Once the IRS has assessed the tax within the assessment statute of limitations as discussed above, the IRS then has 10 years in which to collect the tax. There are certain events that can extend the statutory period past the 10-year mark, because they actually "stop the clock". These events include:

- filing bankruptcy

- filing certain appeal requests

- entering into litigation with the IRS

- filing an Offer in Compromise

- filing a request for an Installment Agreement

- requesting a military deferment

- filing an innocent spouse defense

With these actions, the statute of limitations is temporarily suspended while that action is being investigated.

The date of assessment is the date the Assessment

Officer signs the Summary Record of Assessment. This information can be verified by obtaining an IRS account transcript called a Record of Account, which you can request from the IRS at any time. If the Summary Record of Assessment was not properly recorded, then the assessment is actually not proper. Some penalties have a different assessment date from that of the original tax. In those cases the penalty has a separate Collection Statute Expiration Date (CSED), which is the date that the 10-year period ends.

The IRS can use administrative or judicial methods to collect delinquent taxes. The IRS generally precedes administratively by levying and seizing assets that you own. If the IRS embarks upon this course of action, the levy must occur within the 10-year statute of limitations period. The IRS can also precede judicially by filing a lawsuit against you within the 10-year limitation period.

During a period of time in which an Installment Agreement request is pending with the IRS, the statute of limitations on collections is suspended for a while. The period is 30 days following a rejection of a proposed Installment Agreement or 30 days following the termination of an Installment Agreement.

The statute of limitations on collections is also suspended during an Offer in Compromise investigation. During the time that the IRS is considering your Offer in Compromise, the statute of limitations clock isn't running. It is also not running for the 30 days following the rejection of an Offer in Compromise.

The situation is similar for bankruptcy. A bankruptcy petition prohibits the IRS from assessing or collecting a claim from you which arose prior to the bankruptcy petition being filed. During this period the assessment limitations period – the three- and six-year period as discussed earlier – is suspended, plus a period of 60 days after the discharge of your bankruptcy. The limitation period for collection is suspended during your bankruptcy petition period and for an additional six months after the bankruptcy is discharged.

There are times where an Appeals Officer is involved in your case. The settlement authority of an Appeals Officer is very broad. However, their primary job is to resolve the tax issue expeditiously and to weigh the costs of potential litigation for the IRS.

The appeals process is one where professional negotiation skills can really come in handy. Since the appeals process relies so much upon negotiation, a high percentage of cases are resolved here. It is not uncommon for those of us that are professional tax resolution representatives to simply resolve our clients' cases in the appeals process rather than relying on a field Revenue Officer to work with us.

The biggest thing that you need to remember is that the

first step in the collection process is for the IRS to actually assess the tax. Until this occurs, the IRS cannot act to collect on that tax. An assessment is simply what the IRS claims you owe. The most common forms of assessment are summary assessments and deficiency assessments.

Summary assessment will usually represent the amount reflected on a tax return that you filed, whereas a deficiency assessment can occur due to an adjustment being made to a filed tax return, such as the result of an audit, or when the IRS files a Substitute for Return.

If you have questions or concerns regarding an IRS assessment, the best thing you can do is speak with a federally licensed taxpayer representative. Please feel free to call my office at (515) 986-5843.

Chapter 6: Understanding IRS Collections And The Resolution Process

The U.S. Internal Revenue Service is the single largest collections agency in the world. In 2010, the IRS spent over $12.5 billion and employed just under 95,000 people to collect more than $2.3 trillion in tax revenue. Of these 95,000 personnel, over 20,000 are directly involved in enforced collections action against taxpayers that owe back taxes.

Needless to say, this is a bill collector that can have a serious impact on your life, especially given the collections actions they can take that other bill collectors can't.

It is important to understand that the IRS is a slow moving bureaucracy that is highly resistant to change, and is heavily driven by forms and written procedures. This doesn't bode well when it comes to fixing your tax problem quickly, but it does provide a major benefit to working to resolve your tax problem: Their playbook is public record, and they're required to follow it.

Here in this chapter, I'm going to provide you an overview of the flow of the IRS collections process and the tax resolution process. Both processes have a very logical, linear flow. In the chapters that follow, we will discuss specific aspects of the tax resolution process, so that you can jump to the chapter and section that is specifically applicable to you, based on where you are in the linear flow of IRS collections.

Collections Starts With A Tax Deficiency

The IRS doesn't start collections activity against you simply because you file a tax return with a balance due and don't pay it. In fact, the collections process really doesn't even start when the tax assessment is made.

In all reality, the IRS collections process begins with a letter called the Statutory Notice of Deficiency (SNOD). Within the industry, we also refer to this as the "21 day letter". This letter is kicked out by a computer automatically when your "number comes up".

This can actually be substantially after your tax return was filed. For individuals that file their tax return on time (by April 15th), it's not uncommon to get the SNOD two to four months after the end of tax season. For business that are behind on payroll taxes, I've seen cases where it take an entire year before the IRS kicks out the SNOD. This delay has been one of the primary things reported by the Taxpayer Advocate to Congress as a major problem within the IRS.

The SNOD is referred to as the 21-day letter because it gives you 21 days in which to pay the tax before additional penalties and interest will accrue on the tax liability. Nothing "bad" is going to happen to you during this period.

Notice of Federal Tax Lien Filing (Form 668-Y)

If you fail to pay your tax bill during the 21-day period of the SNOD, don't set up a payment plan, and don't contest the validity of the tax bill, then the next automatic step, again performed by a computer, is the filing of a Notice of Federal Tax Lien (NFTL). Under new rules issued in February 2011, the IRS will only file an actual tax lien against you if your total tax debt exceeds $10,000, including any prior years you may owe for.

As discussed earlier, a tax lien attaches to everything you own, including your wages and all your property. In addition, a tax lien is eventually indicated on your credit report, and can impact you in numerous ways, also discussed in the earlier chapter on tax liens.

Notice of Intent to Levy (Form Letter CP-504)

Approximately 30 to 45 days after the filing of an actual tax lien, a computer will again kick out another notice to you. This notice will be titled "Notice of Intent to Levy" and contain a designation in the upper right or lower right corner labeled "CP-504".

When you receive a CP-504, it is important to know one major thing: It has no teeth. It is a letter required to be sent to you by law, to notify you that, because of the tax lien, the IRS has the authority to take serious collections action against, such as levies. In reality, the letter itself doesn't grant any rights to either you or the IRS, but when you receive it, it's important to mark it on the calendar, because 30 days after the CP-504, you're going to get something much, much more important.

Final Notice of Intent to Levy (Letter 1058)

Exactly 30 days after a CP-504 is issued, you're going to get another form letter from the IRS, labeled "Final Notice of Intent to Levy". In the upper right or lower right corner will be "Letter 1058".

Letter 1058 is important for two reasons:

1. It is the first opportunity you have to file an Appeal.

2. Thirty days after this letter, the IRS can actually levy you.

Here's the bottom line thing to understand about the Letter 1058: If you don't file an Appeal of this notice, the IRS *can* initiate levy action 30 days after they send this notice. In other words, you can safely ignore a lien and a CP-504, but you simply can't ignore a Letter 1058.

Does a Letter 1058 mean that the IRS *will* levy you? No, it doesn't, particularly if they don't have the information necessary to issue a levy. For example, if they don't know where you bank and don't know where you work, they can't very well issue a levy. However, if you still work at the same job that you had when you filed the tax return, the IRS knows where you work, because they received a copy of your W-2 from your employer. Also, if you have in the past given the IRS your bank account number and bank routing number in order to have a refund direct deposited, then they know where your bank is.

Whenever you receive a Letter 1058, you should file an Appeal. In order to do this, file Form 12153, *Request for Collection Due Process Appeal*. Further information about filing this appeal, called a "CDP" for short, is available in the Appeals chapter, later in this book. Normally, in my practice I will file a CDP appeal about 20 days into the 30 day window for doing so, in order to give my client as much time as possible to get their finances in order.

The Cycle Repeats

The cycle of SNOD → NFTL → CP-504 → Letter 1058 repeats itself any time you incur a new tax liability. For individual taxpayers, that means this cycle could repeat itself once per year. For a business dealing with employment taxes, this cycle could basically never end, since payroll tax returns are filed quarterly, and this cycle takes about 4 months to complete.

Revenue Officer Assignment

Your first time through this cycle, your case will exist within a division of the IRS called the Automated Collection System (ACS). ACS personnel are located at several of the largest IRS service centers, including Ogden, UT, Cincinnati, OH, and Philadelphia, PA. The majority of letters you receive from the IRS will be from one of these service centers.

Unless your collections case has special circumstances associated with it, you will usually stay assigned to ACS even if you accumulate two or three year's worth of tax debt as an individual, or 3 or 4 quarters of payroll tax liability for a business. After reaching this threshold, your case will likely be assigned to a Revenue Officer. Revenue Officers (RO) are field agents that live and work in local community all over the United States. There are currently over 14,000 of these personnel working for the IRS.

An interesting thing about the current economic situation is that there are a growing number of taxpayers falling into trouble with the IRS. Because of this, the waiting line for assignment to an RO is many areas of the country is growing longer and longer. Certain taxpayers are bumped ahead of the line, depending on their circumstances. But for most taxpayers, they are waiting longer and longer, which gives them more and more time to get their finances in order and hopefully be able to work out something once they *do* get assigned to a field agent.

I've mentioned several times that there are certain circumstances that will get you assigned to a Revenue Officer much faster. Some of those circumstances include:

- your total tax debt is particularly large

- you have personal tax debt for 3+ years

- you owe payroll taxes and are not actively making Federal Tax Deposits

When you are assigned to a Revenue Officer, the course of your tax case takes a sudden shift for the worse. This is the point at which it is definitely advisable to bring in professional representation to assist you.

The Tax Resolution Process

Whether your case is still assigned to ACS, or if it's been assigned to a Revenue Officer, there is a fairly standard, step-by-step process by which your tax case gets resolved. Since the IRS has their own procedures that employees have to follow, you can always know what the next action from the IRS Collections division is going to be.

In general, these are the steps that you will need to follow to make progress towards a successful and permanent tax resolution:

1. Contact ACS or your Revenue Officer and negotiate a time period of 30 to 120 days in order to get your affairs in order for resolving your tax situation.

2. File appeals on any items which you are eligible to do so.

3. File all past due tax returns, including replacing SFR's.

4. Complete a Collection Information Statement, including supporting documentation, to determine your current financial condition.

5. Determine the best resolution strategy based on your financial condition.

6. Apply for and negotiate towards the chosen resolution strategy.

7. Go through the Appeals process, if necessary.

8. Apply for a penalty abatement, if necessary.

These are the same big picture steps that I follow myself when working with a client.

Jim McClaflin, EA

Chapter 7: Offer In Compromise Program

Whenever you hear the phrase "pennies on the dollar" in relation to tax resolution, you are hearing a reference to the Offer in Compromise (OIC) program.

The OIC program is intended to give taxpayer's without the financial means to pay their tax debt to pay whatever they have, and then start over. In many ways, an OIC is akin to a bankruptcy filing on taxes only

An Offer in Compromise application will require complete financial disclosure, along with *complete* supporting documentation. Because the government is going to accept less money for the tax debt than what you owe, they are going to go to great lengths to make sure that you actually qualify. Refer back to the recordkeeping chapter of this book for more information about the types of information the IRS would expect you to produce in these situations.

Eligibility

Your eligibility to settle for less than what you owe is directly related to your offer amount. If your offer amount is equal to or greater than the minimum amount calculated using the IRS formula, then you may be eligible to file an Offer in Compromise.

Like other resolution options, the IRS also requires that you:

- have filed all past due tax returns

- are not currently generating new tax liabilities

- agree to properly file and pay on all tax returns, on time, for the next 5 years

- agree to let the IRS keep any tax refunds you would otherwise be due during the time you are paying on the OIC

Failure to abide by these rules will either result in rejection of your offer, or default of your offer agreement and reinstatement of any tax liabilities that were eliminated.

Payment Options

In addition to a small application fee, you are required to make payments on the Offer in Compromise unless you meet low income qualification guidelines for an exception to this rule.

The first payment option is used when you will pay the entire amount of your settlement offer in 5 monthly payments or less. If you use this option, you may pay the entire offer amount when submitting your application, or include a minimum 20% deposit (non-refundable!) and take up to a maximum of 5 more monthly payments to pay off your offer. Using this payment option provides the benefit of not being required to make regular payments on your Offer while it is being processed. Using this option also generally results in paying the smallest possible Offer amount.

The second payment option requires you to make regular monthly payments on your Offer in Compromise while the IRS is considering it. These payments are non-refundable, and the first payment needs to be included with your offer application. This second payment option allows up to 24 months to pay the full amount of your Offer.

Regardless of the payment option you use, your payments must add up to the total offer amount, and your offer amount must be at least your Reasonable Collection Potential (RCP), discussed next.

Keep in mind that penalties and interest continue to build on your tax liability while you make Offer payments, even though ultimately those penalties and interest go away when the Offer is paid off and settled. If you default on your OIC, however, those built up penalties and interested are added back on to your balance and you will be liable for them.

Offer Calculation

Many unlicensed tax resolution salespeople, either through ignorance or simply gross incompetence, will tell everybody that they talk to that they qualify for an OIC, and that the Offer amount is some percentage of what they owe.

In addition to this horrifically unethical practice, many tax resolution firms will also only tout their most successful OIC applications, showing you that they did indeed get 1.2 cents on the dollar for one client, and 4 cents on the dollar for another client, all while failing to inform you that:

> a. Most of their OIC applications for clients were outright rejected, and

> b. of those that were accepted, it was usually only for 50 or 75 cents on the dollar.

The Offer amount is the single most important part of a successful OIC application. Calculating the OIC offer amount is extremely formulaic, and requires a complete and accurate Form 433 to be filled out. The IRS goes through an extensive investigation phase to verify information on your Form 433, looking for other assets you own and income you failed to disclose. The IRS looks at various public records sources, and may even pull a credit report to verify what you've told them (this action doesn't require your direct authorization to the

IRS under Federal law).

Within the IRS booklet containing the OIC application, there are versions of the Form 433-A and Form 433-B that are modified slightly for OIC purposes. If you use the PDF version of the booklet (search for "IRS Form 656B"), the calculations are actually carried forward for you to the lines that determine your Offer amount.

The entire purpose of these calculations is to arrive at what the IRS calls your "Reasonable Collection Potential", or RCP. The RCP is the sum of the net worth of your assets plus all of your disposable income for the next 1 or 2 years. In other words:

Settlement Amount = (monthly disposable income x 12 or 24 months) + the net realizable equity in the taxpayer's assets)

Disposable income is monthly income minus allowable monthly expenses. It is important to recognize that the IRS will not allow all expenses that you may actually have. Common disallowed expenses are college tuition payments for your children and credit card payments beyond your minimum payment.

The number of months over which disposable income must be calculated into the offer amount is based on the payment plan option you've chosen. If you're paying the Offer on the 5-month plan, then your remaining income is multiplied by 12. If you're paying on the 6 to 24 month plan, then your remaining income is multiplied by 24. Therefore, it at all possible, it obviously behooves you to choose the 5-month payment plan if you can swing it.

"Net realizable equity in assets" is the quick sale value of the asset (often 80% of Fair Market Value (FMV)) minus any liabilities which are secured by the asset (e.g., a loan). As an example, if a taxpayer has a home worth $100,000 and owes $50,000 on the home, the IRS will calculate the net realizable equity in the asset as follows: ($100,000 x .80) - $50,000 = $30,000. The IRS expects, in this example, that the $30,000 will be included in the Offer amount.

Based on this explanation of how RCP is determined, and understanding that RCP is your minimum offer amount, I hope it is apparent as to why the IRS rejects so many OIC applications. In reality, the best OIC candidates are folks that have very little in the way of assets, and no disposable income. The best OIC candidates often tend to be unemployed and broke.

Application Process – What To Expect

When you file an OIC, a Process Examiner will look over your paperwork to make sure that the Offer application meets all the administrative requirements to be eligible, including properly filled out forms, a complete Form 433, and no unfiled tax returns.

Then, an Offer Examiner will be assigned to actually review the merits and financial aspects of your application. This is the person that verifies assets, orders credit reports, and basically gets very up close and personal regarding every aspect of your financial situation or the financial health of your business.

The Offer Examiner will usually provide you the opportunity to address any inconsistencies they discover in their findings, and to argue on your own behalf for the inclusion or exclusion of certain assets or expenses. More often than not, this is the phase where having a professional representative comes in handy the most, to handle these negotiations for you.

Once the Offer Examiner has all the information they need to either accept or reject your Offer, they will do so, and send you a letter explaining why.

Keep in mind that for Payment Option 2, you must continue to make monthly payments on your OIC while this review process is going on.

If you fail to do so, your offer will automatically be rejected, and the IRS will keep the money you did pay and apply it to your tax liability as they see fit.

Appeals

If your OIC is rejected, you have the right to know why, and also the right to Appeal this decision. More often than not, a dispute over including an asset or expense item will be the argument you take to Appeals. Appeals Officers have the authority to accept or reject an OIC based on their own findings, rather than the findings of the Offer Examiner.

Professional Representation

I've said it before in this book, and I'll say it again: *Certain IRS processes really do necessitate professional representation.*

This is obviously one of them. Whether you need help in calculating your RCP, have been denied a legitimate Offer in Compromise application, or are lost on filing your initial application, let me help. Call my office at (515) 986-5843 for assistance in any of these matters.

Chapter 8: Reducing IRS Penalties With Reasonable Cause Penalty Abatements

There are a lot of common misconceptions surrounding the abatement (removal) of IRS penalties and interest.

First of all, it is important for anybody that owes the IRS money to understand that you will not have interest charges removed. If somebody is trying to sell you on their tax relief services and they tell you that they can have the amount of interest on your tax account reduced or eliminated, they're lying. The provisions within the U.S. tax code for eliminating interest charges on back taxes are extremely limited and extremely specific, and if you owe the money but just simply couldn't or didn't pay it, you DO NOT qualify.

The second thing to understand is that the removal of any penalties is extremely formulaic. You must meet one of the reasonable cause criteria outlined by the Internal Revenue Code. Fortunately, these reasonable cause criteria are much broader and more applicable to more people and businesses than are the criteria for interest abatement. Some of the possible reasonable cause criteria include death or illness in the family, loss of records, and receiving bad advice from a CPA.

It is important to note that the two most common causes

for accrual of a tax liability are not considered reasonable cause by the IRS, and most often you will not be able to have penalties reduced for these two reasons. These reasons are:

1. Ignorance of filing or deposit requirements

2. Cash flow problems that leave you without enough money to pay the tax when due

Under special circumstances, the IRS will grant penalty relief due to economic hardship, but it is a hard case to prove and tends to be a longer, more drawn out process through the Appeals division. The granting of this sort of penalty relief can also depend upon which Circuit Court of Appeals district you live in, since different case law has been interpreted in a different court jurisdictions.

Above all, just remember that you can get penalties abated, if you have a good reason that was beyond your control and that can be backed up with proper documentation. And as far as interest charges go – forget about it, the IRS is not going to let you off the hook for those if you actually do owe the tax.

One of the biggest things I am adamant about is correcting the myths, lies, and half-truths perpetuated by unlicensed tax resolution salespeople, and the IRS penalty abatement is one of the things least understood and grossly over-hyped by salespeople in our industry.

The "we can remove interest charges" lie, as mentioned at the start of this chapter, is one of the biggest lies that tax resolution sales people tell their propsects.

There are two, and precisely two, instances in which interest is reduced:

1. An IRS employee gives you false information, which you acted on and resulted in the interest. This is one reason why all IRS correspondence should be conducted and followed up in writing.

2.Since interest is calculated based on the tax liability, if an amended return is filed and the tax itself is lowered, then the interest is also reduced.

Reasonable Cause Criteria

Now, on to penalties. The IRS charges dozens of different types of penalties, but the three that we most commonly talk about are the late filing penalty, the late payment penalty, and the penalty for not making Federal Tax Deposits. These three penalties combined can add a whopping 65% to your total IRS bill. If your tax debt is more than two years old, you've maxed out all these penalties, and therefore over half your total debt is penalties.

The IRS does actually have a compassionate side, and

it's generally found in the penalty abatement process. Penalty abatement applications can also be appealed if initially denied, so you can always get a second set of eyeballs on the issue. The thing to keep in mind is that the IRS has very strict guidelines for granting penalty abatements, and these guidelines are referred to as "reasonable cause criteria".

As mentioned earlier, "we didn't have the money" is NOT a reasonable cause criteria. A drop in revenue, by itself, is insufficient argument for obtaining penalty relief. Any request for penalty abatement simply citing the economic recession will be immediately denied.

Why is this? Here is the IRS' logic: You made the money, and should have paid the taxes at the time on that money. If you are self-employed and receive a check, then you HAD the money, you simply didn't give the IRS their chunk of it. Same goes with payroll taxes for businesses, particularly the trust fund taxes (money you withhold from employee paychecks for income tax and Medicare/Social Security): If you had the expectation to pay some amount of wage, then you theoretically HAD the money sitting somewhere to pay that person, and should have withheld it and turned it over to the IRS. If you couldn't cover the taxes, you shouldn't have had the employee and should have laid people off or cut back their hours.

There are ways to argue around this, and we have done

so very successfully, but there has to be some other circumstance. For example, you had the money to pay the tax, but paying the tax instead of something else would have created an "undue hardship".

Examples of "undue hardship" could include a large medical expense that unpaid would have left a condition untreated, or a court ordered payment that, if missed, would have resulted in other legal consequences, or a bill such as a large automobile repair which would have left you unable to get to work and resulted in job loss.

These arguments are difficult to make and require significantly more work than standard reasonable cause criteria applications, but they CAN be won, especially in the Appeals process.

The primary IRS penalty abatement reasonable cause criteria center around natural disasters, loss or destruction of vital business records, bad advice from the IRS or an accounting professional, criminal activity, medical issues, substance abuse problems, and other serious circumstances.

A couple years ago I developed a standard list of questions to ask clients to assist me in preparing their penalty abatement. This list of questions should be given some serious thought before requesting penalty abatement, as you are more likely to get what you want if your request covers one of these areas:

- Were any financial records lost or destroyed?

- Was there any transition in your business that lead to the failure to pay taxes, such as a change of ownership?

- Was there a death or serious illness that directly affected your ability to work or impacted the operation of your business?

- Were you the victim of any embezzlement of funds, theft of valuable property, or identity theft?

- Were there any alcohol or drug abuse issues that affected your business or your personal wage earning capability?

- Was there a natural disaster that impacted you or your business?

- Did you rely on the advice of a CPA or IRS employee in making tax decisions?

- Were there any circumstances that created substantial financial hardship, to the point where either yourself or your business was close to going bankrupt?

These questions cover all of the IRS reasonable cause criteria to one extent or another, so finding an answer to your personal or business situation that covers one or more of these questions is the key to a successful penalty abatement application.

Writing Your Penalty Abatement Request

You <u>can</u> use Form 843, *Claim for Refund and Request for Abatement* to apply for relief from penalties. However, as a tax practitioner, I never have, not even once. The reason is simply because the form only has room for about two sentences in order to explain WHY you are requesting the penalties to be removed. Therefore, you're going to end up writing a lengthy letter anyway that gets attached to the Form 843. Because of this, I simply write a letter for my clients that includes all the same information as the Form 843. My typical penalty abatement letter is 3 to 5 pages long, and some are even longer.

The format of a penalty abatement letter is fairly straightforward. When requesting a penalty abatement, I suggest the following format:

1. Indicate the particular penalty types, tax periods, and penalty amounts that you are requesting to be reduced or removed.

2. Include a very brief introduction about who you are, where you live, your family size, and what

you do. For a business, give a very brief description of your business, what it does, and how it does it.

3. Provide the background story to the event that caused the tax bills to go unpaid. Be sure to include very specific details, including names, dates, places, events, etc.

4. After explaining why the taxes weren't paid, explain what actions you took to correct the situation, including an explanation regarding the length of time it took to get the tax situation addressed.

5. For business taxes, explain why other business expenses were paid when the taxes were not.

6. Explain the current state of affairs, including the current status of your personal or business finances, and also the status of meeting your current tax obligations and how you've addressed the back tax liabilities

7. Sign your request under penalties of perjury.

Where To Send Penalty Abatement Requests

If you have or recently had a Revenue Officer assigned to you, send your penalty abatement request to that Revenue Officer.

If you do not have a Revenue Officer: Most of your IRS notices most likely come from one particular IRS service center. Make note of the address of that IRS center, and mail your request their to the attention of "Service Center Penalty Appeals Coordinator".

Penalty Abatement Review Process

Whether it is a Revenue Officer or the service center coordinator that reviews your request, they will make a determination regarding whether they believe your request meets reasonable cause criteria.

If it is determined that your application meets reasonable cause criteria, the person reviewing your request will recommend removal of penalties for certain types and period, based on your circumstances. This recommendation will then be forwarded to a manager for final approval.

If your request is denied, you will be told so in writing. You are entitled to know the exact reason that your request was denied. If you are not supplied with this reason in the initial rejection letter, then you should call or write to that person to request it.

All penalty abatement denials have appeals rights. If your penalty abatement is denied for any reason, be sure that you exercise this right. Call our office at (515) 986-5843 if you need assistance with this appeal process, we'd be more than happy to help you with it.

Jim McClaflin, EA

This Book Is Just The Beginning

This book is intended to be just the beginning of a long and healthy relationship between the two of us. I'd like to invite you to visit my website at

www.DesMoines-Tax.com

and receive my free report, *The Top 7 Small Business Strategies For Increasing Profits in a Recession Recovery*. We'll also keep in touch with you on a regular basis-offering **Real World Personal Strategies** (*not just pie-in-the-sky theory*) and guidance for growing wealth, keeping sane in this world, and all-around personal development.

These will NOT be just *tax tips* (it's our job to take care of all that for you, after all). Sure, there will be tax items you'll need to know about that we'll send you info on, but I believe you'll find these notes to be interesting and useful on a variety of levels. Oh, and it's free.

Jim McClaflin, EA

About The Author

Enrolled Agent Jim McClaflin is a federally licensed taxpayer representative. He is a member of the National Association of Tax Professionals and the National Association of Enrolled Agents. His firm, Accounting & Tax Professionals, PLC, is a member of the Grimes, IA Chamber of Commerce and maintains an A+ rating with the Better Business Bureau.

Team up with Jim today. You'll wish you had done so sooner. Visit www.DesMoines-Tax.com or call (515) 986-5843 to connect with Jim today.

www.ingramcontent.com/pod-product-compliance
Lightning Source LLC
Chambersburg PA
CBHW051331170526
45166CB00002B/770